A Mother's Love / A Mother's Pain

Latricia Taylor

Copyright © 2018 Latricia N. Taylor

All rights reserved.

ISBN:0692089349
ISBN-13: 978-0692089347
Front & Back cover designed by: Shanna Williams-Prater, Reanna Prints

DEDICATION

A Mother's Love / A Mother's Pain is dedicated and inspired by the love in memory of my daughter, Chasity S. M. Taylor, who became an Angel on November 2, 2014. I also dedicate this book to all mothers who lost their child/children unexpectedly in any type of tragedy. I pray my experience is able to help at least one mother walk the journey that no mother should ever walk in her life.

CONTENTS

Dedication

Preface

Acknowledgement   vii

Introduction   Pg. #9

1   Love   Pg. #10

2   Pain   Pg. #22

3   Journey   Pg. #34

4   New Normal   Pg. #38

Letters to my Daughter   Pg. #46

Journal   Pg. #51

Preface

After the loss of my daughter, many people advise that I should write down my thoughts and write a letter if necessary to my daughter. I started, but couldn't get myself to take my thoughts and add it to paper. However, I continue to have thoughts formulate in my mind of what I wanted to say if I had one last time to speak with her. These thoughts haunted me night after night, and I could not sleep. These thoughts were bottled up, and I finally decided to take them and place them in book form. I figured that I am not alone on this journey and maybe my words could help or encourage someone else.

ACKNOWLEDGMENTS

I want to take the time to acknowledge those families and friends who were there from day one and have been truly by my side every day since. I won't name everyone, but I will say a special THANK YOU and I LOVE YOU to my husband, Eugene, and my son, D'Andre. Most people only see me when I am able to put my "I am okay" face on in public. These two have seen the pain in my eyes, the days I didn't want to get out of bed, the tears I cry daily, and they love me and held me up when I couldn't hold myself together. For that, I truly love them for that and continue being by my side. The loss of Chasity was hard for us and many others, but the pain was tripled when we look into the eyes of the daughter she left behind and understood one day we would need to sit down and explain to her where heaven really is and that her mother is never coming back. I want to say Thank you to my mom, Barbara. My mom experienced the same type of loss eight years prior when my brother was killed. When I didn't understand how to feel, I would give her a call, and she would share with me how she dealt with things, which helped me push through as well. Thank you to my daughter, Shamara; I could not comfort her or D'Andre as their mother because I was too broken. But she understood and stepped up as well and was always a phone call away to listen when I was angry and wanted to share some choice words with some people. She reminded me that some people aren't worth my energy. I appreciate all of these people that I was able to lean on during this journey.

In addition, I want to say THANK YOU to The Chasity Taylor Foundation board. Each and every one of them has been right by my side with just as much love and passion, making the Foundation the best we can make it for the youth in the community and to honor Chasity. Myra, Horace, Violet, Ashlea, Heather, and Jarrod, Thank you!!!

I pray everyone enjoys the book, and I thank you in advance for taking the time to read my book and have an open mind to what is written.

"To get up when you are down, to fight more intensely when you are struggling; to put in the extra effort when you are in sheer pain, to come back when nobody expects you to, and to stand tall when everyone is pulling you down are what makes a champion."

-Apoorve Dubey

Introduction

This book is about a mother's journey into motherhood and transitioning into the pain of losing a child and how I am able to cope daily with the pain. It was important to share with everyone my journey and how I am able to stand during a time I should have given up on life. This book will connect with some individuals with same or similar experiences and provide insight to others who have not gone through the same journey. It's a motivational book. I pray this book will give hope and encouragement to the individuals that are struggling with grief, sorrow, or life pain in general of losing a child.

The journey of writing this book was a process of three years. I wasn't sure how to go about putting my thoughts to paper. I felt lead to write this book, but was having trouble starting because I wasn't sure what others would think of me or if it would reach the right people and help at least one person. The struggle wasn't great, but I managed to push through.

1 LOVE

It has been said that women experience motherhood differently. Some embrace it from the first day they find out they are expecting, others connect once the baby is born, and we do have those that sometimes have a difficult time connecting at all. I am unsure what the reason is for either stage, but I will say it was a joy and pain from the start for me personally. I love my children, but boy oh boy, each one made me cry before they were ever born and, of course, over the years as well. Go figure! Ha

Children bring joy to the world, and as a mother, we are programmed to be nurtures and protectors of our children. Most often, mothers sacrificed everything they have to make sure they can provide the entire child's wants and needs. Mothers love their children unconditionally, and often people don't understand how much pain mothers endure with raising children.

I gave birth to my first child at age 15 (yes, I was a teen mom); I was hurt when I found out I was pregnant because I could not believe I allowed myself to get pregnant at such an early age. This wasn't something my mother ever wanted, neither for me nor did I for myself. But I allowed peer pressure and I, being in love, made a decision that stayed with me forever. No, my child was not meant to be here at that time, but she was never a mistake. I believe it was God giving me something to push me and motivate me to be the best person I could be for my future self. To add insult to injury - This was a difficult time for my family as a few months prior, we lost my grandmother - the rock of our family - and I just knew my mother was just going to kill me for being pregnant. I was in denial for a while, but my godmother encouraged me and kept my mother calm from killing me on sight in the beginning. Ha! However, to be honest, my mom wanted me to have an abortion. She figured having a baby at 15 was not a good thing. I went to all of the pre doctors' appointments; my godmother, Margie, went with me to the appointment that was supposed to be the one to set the date to terminate. Guess what? God had other plans. The doctor, who was a long time doctor of my mom and birthed my little brother so he knew our family well and my mother, trusted him. He sat in that office and told me and my godmother (my mom had to work) that I would have to leave Syracuse to have the procedure and it would not be good on my body because of how far along I was at the time. My godmother made the call to my mother to give her the news. I could hear through the phone, "Oh Hell No! – I'm not putting my child through that." My godmother hung up, turned to me, and said, "Guess what, we are having a baby." She was so excited she took me to lunch. As we sat down to eat, she had a long discussion with me regarding the changes I would go through, what to expect and, to wrap it up, how for me not to give up on my dreams or goals. She made sure to remind me she would be right here for me, as well as my mom. I felt relieved that I had two strong women in my corner, but still disappointed inside that I let my mom and myself down by even being in the situation of being pregnant at age 15. Unfortunately, since we were so young, a real lasting relationship with her dad was not an option. But as teen parents, we did the best we could to co-parent, but without my mother, I would not have gotten through motherhood at such a young age. I vowed I was going to not be just another teen mom. My mother was right there from that day until now. She has always been supportive as ever and still has my back. I truly appreciate her for everything she has done and still do for my kids and me.

At that time, they wanted to send girls like me to special facilities to go to school, so you didn't have to walk around high school and be ashamed of being a teen mom. Well, most girls who did attend these pregnancy-type schools fell behind in their studies, failed or just dropped out. I didn't want any of that to happen to me, and neither did my mom. My mom stood up to the principal, and I went to regular classes with my classmates. My friends were supportive, and they made me feel welcome and normal. I did not turn out to be a statistic of being a teen mom that never graduated. It was hard work. My mother scheduled me a tutor for after I gave birth. Guess who didn't sit home and do nothing for those 6 weeks after birth, me. The next morning after I came home from the hospital, the tutor was at my door at 8:00 am. I worked weekly 2-3 days a week for those 6 weeks with the tutor. My godmother watched the baby while I was with the tutor; I took care of her after tutoring, and my mom watched her when she got off work if I needed to study. I got through that semester and every other semester with A's & B's. I graduated with my class from high school, went to junior college and graduated with skills to allow me to have a great job working at a bank. From there, I ended up working for a huge fortunate 500 company, and this opportunity helped me kick-start my career. As I worked and took care of my daughter 6 years later, I fell in love and became pregnant with my 2nd daughter (Chasity). This was not planned either, but this time I was 21, working a great job, and living on my own.

My 2nd pregnancy was the worst of them all. I had issues from the start. I ended up on bed rest several times starting at 6 months and last time was at 8 months into my pregnancy. I had various tests and was told my daughter would be born with severe Down syndrome. They wanted me to decide to abort her or gain counseling to deal with a child such as this. I prayed and had faith I would have a healthy daughter. I cried and cried, but God answered prayers because I gave birth to a healthy baby girl whose only illnesses in her life was having asthma and allergies. Ha! It was a joy to have 2 healthy girls, as well as family and friends who supported me 100%. I was a proud mother of two, and these little individuals motivated me to do more with my life. I wanted to be a lawyer and wanted to go back to College, but at that time, I didn't think that was an option with two kids. Therefore, I continued to work at my job and made some positive career moves while working at the company. When my youngest turned about 6 months, her dad had this bright idea that I should move to Florida with him so he could be closer to her. We met while he was in the military and he later moved back to Florida prior to me giving birth. Like any young relationships, we had many issues that lead to us not being able to be together, so we felt it was best to co-parent. I thought about it, and as things weren't really doing it for me in my hometown, I took him up on the offer with one condition; I would meet him half-way and live in Jacksonville, FL, which was closer to my uncle and family. I felt better being in a new place if I had a family of my own near me. I took leave from work, packed up my apartment, sold everything in it and took a leap of faith and moved to Florida with my two children.

The move was tough because I was leaving my mother, my brothers, and family I have been around my entire life. But I needed to make a change for myself and my kids, and I thought moving was the step in the right direction. As with anything else, changes come with challenges. I had a rough time establishing employment, getting a place to live, and getting my kids adjusted to new surroundings and new family in their life. However, with those prayers I know my grandmother had stored up on my behalf and my prayers, I begin to see the light. Things started moving well and I push through and never looked back or regret the decision. Life was going well for the kids and me, but as soon as I thought my life and family was complete, something was missing from my life. Although I loved my daughters, my heart hurt for a little boy, but I decided to close the chapter on my childbearing years and be happy with my 2 healthy daughters. Well, they say God is amused when we make our plans and they are different from his plan. Well, 6 years later, I became pregnant again. I was overjoyed, and I prayed that this would be my son. Well, God had other plans; I lost my baby at 4 ½ months, and the doctors could not tell me why. He or she just stops growing inside me and no one had an explanation. I was devasted. I blamed myself no matter what the doctor told me. As a mother, you are your child's protector, and it's your job to protect them the best you can, and I felt I failed the little one that was growing inside me. As I went to have the procedure to deliver this 5-month-old fetus, I felt someone had stabbed me in the heart. But there was nothing I could do to save his or her life. Therefore, I had to move past the situation. No one ever spoke of the situation to me and I always kept it inside. Even to this day, I still wondered if it was a girl or boy and what actually happened. But the pain was bearable and I think it was easier to push the thoughts to the side because I never got to meet the little one and the connection in the womb was cut short. I still had questions with no answers. I was determined I was done, and I would check into getting my tubes tied. I didn't want to experience a lost again, so I was going to be satisfied with just my two girls. However, again, God had other plans, and I found out I was pregnant again a year later. My doctor did a wonderful job to do everything possible to not have a repeat of the year previously. I was treated as high risk; I had many ultrasounds along the way to ensure everything was going well. When I was able to find out the sex and I was told it was a boy, I knew God was on my side. It was the son I always knew I was meant to have and I could not wait to meet him. We begin thinking of names and not knowing why, at the time, I wanted to give him a name similar to my brother. I didn't understand it at the time, but God provided light on it later. In July 2000, I gave birth to a healthy baby boy born three weeks early, and we were so happy. I knew at that time my family was complete. God had a plan, he fulfilled that plan for us, and it felt so good to be a mother of three.

My family has always been supportive and close. I come from a family of 4 children, and I am the only girl stuck somewhere in the middle. My mother made sure to raise us to have a close relationship and remarkable bond as siblings. Yes, we did have normal sibling fights, but nothing that kept us apart from each other. As I stated previously, I was a teen mom and the first out of the group to have children. My brothers were the best uncles. Once they started having children, I was there for them for their children as well. Although I love all my brothers, my brother under me and I had the tighter bond. Hence, the reason I named my son after him.

Well, as life deals you a bad hand, you never want to experience losing a child. Unfortunately, My mother had to experience this pain. Eight years after my son was born, my brother was killed. This became, in my life, the first experience of feeling the part of my heart being ripped out of my chest. I had no clue the pain my mother was feeling. It was devastating and unexpected, and it was a hard pill for our family to swallow. My mother did her best to be brave and strong, but the pain was overwhelming. My son became close to my brother over the years, and my brother had taken a liking to him as well. He loved to share stories with him when we went to my hometown to visit. He would attempt to teach him things he felt as an uncle he should share with him and, of course, spoil him. The day he died, I knew it would be hard, but my son would have those special moments and memories for life as well as everyone else in our family. This was the first time I was on the side of knowing someone personally that lost a child and watched them go through pain like I did my mom. I prayed I would never have to go through the same pain my mother was experiencing.

As the years went on, we were the typical family. School activities, homework, family time, trips, sports activities, etc., and they began to grow up. I watched in amazement how, with every blink of an eye, they were becoming little adults with attitudes (a few more than I bargained for). I was proud of them. They had become three individuals, but had a sibling bond that was warming to the heart. Of course, they had sibling fights, etc., like all other siblings, but they were temporary. Heck, they formed alliances against me if I yelled at one or punished one of them. It was funny how they would go check on each other and ask the famous question "What did she do to you?" Like really, but I would laugh and walk away because I was happy they loved each other and was willing to protect each other at all cost. It was just how I wanted it to be with them. This is the same way my mother raised my brothers and me.

    Motherhood is different for everyone because we all have different backgrounds, with access to different healthcare, finances, and we have different support systems. I was lucky to have a support system (family) that was always there for me and pushed me to continue being the best woman I could be for my kids. Never allowing anyone to put doubt in my mind about who I was or what I was capable of becoming. I always knew I could write my own destiny. I made my own choices and rather they were good or bad, they were my choices to deal with either way. Life throws a lot at a woman and it doesn't matter if you are married, had a father in your life, the child's father is around or not. Women can stand tall and make the best of the situations. The love by a mother for her child is unconditional. A mother's love is a love that one cannot compare to anything. A child is a part of you; when the baby begins forming in your stomach, you begin dreaming about what he or she would look like, the plans you have for them, and you connect from the start. No matter how old the child is, the love for them is the same. A mother wants to and will protect their child at all cost. A mother loves her child despite their flaws because they can see the good in them that no one else can see. A mother sees their child's heart because they listen to each beat from the start of their life. A mother's bond with their child is one like no other, and no one can take that away no matter how much someone tries. A mother can be astray from their child once they become older for various reasons, but one thing that can never change, if the mother raised that child from the start, is the bond formed between mother and child. I feel this is true regardless of the situation. An abusive mother and a drug-addicted mother still feel love for their child; they are showing it in the wrong way, and the child is experiencing it the wrong way. However, if you ask most abusive mothers or drug addicted mothers, they still love that child and wish they could have done things differently to express their love a different way. Motherhood is something women typically learn through watching their mothers growing up, family members or watching other mothers on television. No one provides a manual at the birth of your child and says here you go, now be a mom. We must feel our way through it, and mothers don't always do things right, but they do their best with what they have to work with.

As for me, motherhood started young and was an arduous journey for me, but with love and encouragement from my mother, I was able to feel my way through it. By the time I had my second child, I thought I had the hang of it and one thing I realize is that as long as you have love for your children, everything else will fall into place. I worked hard to provide financial stability for my children, but loving them came easy. I learned how to love my children from the love my mother showed my brothers and I growing up. I would go out of my way to make sure they were protected as much as I could growing up, but still allowing them to be individuals and experience life as children should experience. I was a strict mother because I wanted nothing but the best for them and wanted them to avoid some of the unnecessary mistakes I experience in my life. I couldn't shield them from them all, but I was able to deflect most of the unnecessary life hurts. As my children became older and I watched them develop into young adults, I smiled to myself because when I thought they weren't listening when they were younger, I found out they were and they carried the advice I gave with them. If, as a mother, we are honest with ourselves, we know our children aren't perfect, and when they are out of our eyesight, the world and the only thing they have to cling to is their Faith and the words you instilled in them as a young child test them. A mother must understand that they will try things and experience things we will not agree with, but if we did our part, our children will maneuver through life and come out on top. It is often hard to set our children free because we don't want any danger or harm to come to them, but without experiencing the world, they are unable to become the productive citizen and prosperous adults we want them to become. The world has changed since I had my first child to this day. However, I will not change one thing about how I raised my children because the ups and downs and the love I poured into them I know meant a lot and will guide them through. In addition, I was taught as a young girl from my grandmother to pray. Therefore, I have always prayed over them since they were born and do every day. Because when they are not in my eyesight, I can't protect them and that is not a good feeling. However, when your children reach a certain age, you must trust them and begin to believe they will be okay when they go out into the world. We send them out into the world daily and trust that they will return the same way you sent them.

2 PAIN

My story is just my story. We all have experienced suffering on many different levels and we handle and deal with it in different ways than others. As for me, my suffering actually began in 1999. In December of 1998, I found out I was pregnant. I had two girls and always dreamed and wanted a son. I was excited and nervous at the same time. My first two pregnancies were always listed as high risk for different reasons. Well, as time went on, I was dealing with incredibly weird and crazy morning sickness, or we can say daytime morning sickness. People can set their clocks at work by me after I ate anything in the morning or afternoon. This was something I prayed would go away because it was making my pregnancy miserable. I reached the 4½-month mark and was excited because I was then able to find out the sex of the baby. I couldn't wait for the doctor to tell me it was a boy. Also at this mark, my morning sickness had completely gone away. As my doctor's appointment was about two weeks away, I was feeling good finally and enjoying not being sick and eating what I wanted every day all day. Then the day arrived that I thought I would see a picture of my son. Like always, my appointment was on my lunch, and I was able to run to the doctor and come back to work. Well, my suffering started this day. As I arrive at the doctor's with excitement inside and smiling. I was not prepared for what followed. As I was taken to the patient room to have mine and the baby vitals and normal checkup before my doctor sent me to have the sonogram. The nurse begins doing her thing. I noticed she kept moving the stereoscope around my belly, but not saying anything. Usually, she says strong heartbeat, sounds good, something along those lines. She was quiet and had worry on her face. She excused herself and then my doctor came in and asked me to call my husband because he needed to share some news. This was a Friday, I never forget. Of course, I called him and he came to the doctor's office. The doctor came in, attempted to listen to the heartbeat again, and then performed an ultrasound. He then informed us that the baby no longer had a heartbeat, and based on his measurements, the baby stopped growing. I was in shock; I broke down and cried my heart out that I was making myself sick. The horrible part about it before the doctor would do anything he needed me to go have another blood test on Monday and then come to his office on Tuesday to review and confirm his findings. This meant I had to go all weekend knowing that the baby inside me was no longer living. I thought this would be the worst pain I would ever experience. Losing a baby I never met personally but carried and had formed a bond for the past 4½ months. In addition, I had to return home and act normal around my girls and everyone else. I wasn't ready to share the news that we lost the baby until the doctor confirmed with us on Monday. The next week, the doctor confirmed the news and set me up to deliver the baby since the baby never passed on his or her own. Therefore, I would be asleep and will deliver what was a baby vaginally, but because of the size, a funeral or nothing will be held, it was treated as a miscarriage. I did not think I would mentally recover from the feeling I had at the time. How do you wrap your head around going to the hospital pregnant, but not coming home with a baby? I had to explain to co-workers and family members that they will never meet a baby. How does this affect your emotional, mental stability? I had so many things running through my head and so many unanswered questions. Of course, I asked the doctor what happened. Why did this happen? He ran a test and could not provide any answers to what happened. I had to live with the words that everyone always quotes "God doesn't make any mistakes." At that time, those words comfort me, and I was able to put the pain of that loss behind me and move on, but I suffered in silence. I didn't know if something was wrong with me or did I get punished for something I did. But again, I had two other children, and they needed their mother, so I pushed through with a smile and went on about life. Yes, a year later, I was blessed to get pregnant again and had a beautiful & healthy baby boy.

No matter how many kids a woman has after a miscarriage or stillbirth, she never forgets the one that didn't make it. It's a memory and feeling that is stuck with you for life. You want to count the child when people ask how many kids you have, but you don't want it to be weird when you tried to explain. Most often, if it's not mentioned, we don't discuss it and act as if it did not happen. I had a wonderful support group, and I'm always able to manage through that bump in the road and continue on the path of motherhood. But I always wonder what sex was the baby, what he or she would look like, and all the things that go with remembering the child who became an angel before you met them. Your life changes forever.

November 2, 2014, my life shifted in a way I could never imagine and not sure how I would ever recover. I received a knock on my door at 8:00 am by the police detectives and as tactfully as they can, they informed me my 22-year-old daughter is now deceased. I froze and stared at the detective and asked him, what did you just say? As I stand there holding my 1½-year-old granddaughter (her daughter), he repeated himself. "Ma'am, I hate to inform you that your daughter, Chasity Taylor, was killed in a car accident early this morning." At that moment, I backed up and fell to my knees. I didn't know if I should cry or what to do because I was trying to comprehend what he just said to me. I asked him questions and he gave me responses and I asked him again, Are you sure she isn't in the hospital? I just spoke to her last night. I begged him to take back what he said and tell me she was okay. At that moment, as he stood silent, I could see in his eyes that it was true. I begin to cry hysterically, and I'm not sure how long this went on, but my granddaughter began wiping the tears from my eyes and calling my name "Gigi," and I looked up at her and went numb. I thought to myself, "Tricia, you got to get it together if this is true, this baby needs you." I grabbed her and held her so tight, and the officer realized we were the only two home and asked is there someone I can call to come to the house with us. I couldn't think. As I was numb and could not get up off the floor, he went in my bedroom and got my cellphone. When he gave the phone to me, he asked me again, "Is there someone that can come to the house to be with you," I looked down at my cellphone and replied, How do I call someone to tell them that my daughter was killed and I need you to come to my house? He looked at me and said, "If you dial the number, I will speak for you." I made a few calls, and within 30 minutes, people showed up. The detectives were a blessing because they stayed right there with my granddaughter and I until someone arrived to be with us and he could explain to them what happened. See, he told me what happened, but I couldn't hear him at that time, I instantly went into another world where nothing he said was true. I didn't want to believe it and refuse to believe what he said to me. I insisted on seeing my daughter, but because they said she died on the scene, she was taken straight to the morgue, and I would not be able to see her until I assigned a funeral home to retrieve her body. Let's say my daughter left my house on November 1, 2014, and was perfectly fine. My last text from her was about 10:30 pm and she was fine. But on November 2, 2104, at 8:30 am, I was told last night was the last time I would see her again because she was gone forever. In addition, I had to share this information with my other children, family, and try to explain to her daughter who is asking for her mommy that she will never see her again. That didn't sit well with me, and I was unable to process anything anyone was saying to me. I was then told I had to plan a funeral for my 22-year-old daughter. I pleaded to GOD that they got that wrong and she was in the hospital with the other two young ladies. That was not a pill I was ready to swallow.

November 2, 2014, began a life of suffering for me as a person. I don't take away anyone else's pain or how they feel or dealing with the loss of my daughter. Everyone bond with her is special and everyone will deal differently. However, I truly feel that a Mother suffers when she loses a child. The suffering is different at each stage of the loss. Therefore, I only can speak from my stages of pain and suffering. When I miscarried at 4½ months, the pain was different. I questioned God, and I challenged myself differently. After the miscarriage, I knew a piece of my heart was gone, but the pain was less painful. I cried and wondered how could this happen. However, there wasn't any real suffering. I was okay with hearing the doctor say, "this has happened to others," "you're not alone," and "you will be okay." All of those words seemed to comfort me in a way I could deal with that loss. I was ready to put it past me and, within time, try again. Not that I was thinking of replacing the child I lost, but the bond with that child wasn't as connected because I never got to hear the heartbeat, I never got to know the gender, or feel him or her move. Well, when the smoke cleared after laying my daughter to rest on November 9th, 2014, the pain intensified for this was when the suffering truly began. I struggled and still struggle with the reality of her being gone. No, I don't walk around truly believing she is alive. But I have created a fantasy world and, in that world, I am waiting for her to walk in the door with her smiling self and say "mommy" like only she can say it. I have gone through every stage of emotions from sad, angry, depressed, but I am stuck in a weird place. I am stuck in a place where I am trying to move about life with a smile and function like everyone wants me to do, but my mind and soul is lost. My heart aches daily and I try to cope with the pain internally without bothering others. The first 2½ years, I cried daily in my car, at work, in the shower, and every time I went to her gravesite. I think I have cried so much my tear ducts are dried up. I started telling myself, "If you don't get it together, people are going to think something is wrong with you." "Your family needs you." "Get it together, people expect you to be okay by now." This made my suffering worst because I didn't know how to completely turn off the pain. Then one day it came to me, "Suffer in silence and no one will ever know." The day I decided to do that, my tears became less, the smiles came about easier, and my speech was different. I thought to myself I am doing this (it was like learning to ride a bike for the first time) and I was happy that I was able to fool everyone and no one has to feel sorry for me anymore. Well, I learned very quickly that was a false sense of security that I developed. My body continued the suffering process internally.

A Mother's Love / A Mother's Pain

According to Merriam Webster (Since 1828), suffering is pain that is caused by injury, illness, loss, etc.: physical, mental, or emotional pain. Most people go through a period of suffering in their life. What I found out through my suffering is that pretending to be well on the outside causes internal sickness. During this time of me trying to fake it until I make it, my internal body was suffering as well. I began having chest pains, severe headaches, and became an insomniac. These things have taken a toll on my body because I am fighting to not show how much pain I am still in to others on the outside. The pain is so real and often people don't understand how 3 years, 10 years, or 20 years after the loss of a child a mother can still be suffering. The bond between a mother and their child begins in the womb. Once a mother hears that first heartbeat, feels that first flutter, and that first kick an instant, a bond begins to form with the child. Giving birth is a bittersweet moment for a mother because she is ready to finally meet the child she carried for 9 months, but the pain of giving birth is unforgettable. However, most women are willing to experience this remarkable feeling of childbirth, at least once in their lifetime. The connection to your child is unbelievably wonderful. God blessed me to witness and experience full-term birth for 3 of the 4 of my children, and I was thankful. However, as I continue to deal with the loss of my daughter, I had to continue to make many ER visits and doctor visits. I tried to convince myself that everything I am dealing with isn't directly related to me still mourning my daughter. I had several uncontrollable meltdowns, weekly anxiety attacks, and I'm sure a few panic attacks. I have awakened in the middle of the night (once I finally went to sleep), sweating and crying. If you can think of it, I went through the emotional/mental fight with myself. I talked to some but not many about what I was experiencing, but most got quiet and just stared at me as if they didn't understand my problem. Therefore, I stopped sharing and continue to smile to make them feel good about being around me. I tried drinking alcohol every night to cope because I didn't want to dream, just more of pass out. Well, one day, I was tired of hurting inside, I was tired of feeling the way I was feeling, and I was tired of not being able to be myself on the outside and express how I was feeling. I made an appointment with my doctor to finally go with the statistics and agree to take depression medicine to stop the thoughts, to stop the pain and just sleep like a normal person. The day came for my appointment and as I went through the regular routine questions and etc. with the nurse, she asked me "what are you here for?" I paused and quietly lowered my head and said, "I need depression medication." The nurse looked at me and said okay and walked out of the room. I felt so horrible after saying that out loud. I thought to myself "is this what life has come to? The very thing I dislike all my life and that's taking medication and I am about to sign up voluntarily to take medication that I may need for the rest of my life. As I sat waiting for the doctor 10 minutes past, and when she came into the room, she said, "How are you feeling today?" I hysterically began to cry. I mean I even started hyperventilating. My doctor is so sweet, bless her heart she handed me tissues and said I will give you all the time you need. I got myself together and apologize for my outburst. She said, "If you don't want to end up in the hospital, you must let her go." I looked at her and tried to pretend I didn't understand what she meant. I let my daughter go; I acknowledge she is gone every time I visit her gravesite. But my doctor could see I was still in denial and trying to pretend that I was okay. She said, it is okay, she will always be with you, but she does not want you to suffer any longer. I began to cry again and told her, but I am not sure what to do with my feelings. I don't know how to let her go. I don't want to take pills. What should I do? My doctor told me she understood my need for not wanting to take the medication and was willing to work with me on things that could help reduce what I was feeling, but I had to promise her that if things don't get better, I must consider medication. I agreed. She told me how proud she was of me for fighting through my emotions without running to medication. She respected my decision and wanted to do any and everything possible to help me stop suffering and use other alternatives than medication to get my body back on track. She suggested I write a book on my experience and I am doing just that.

For those mothers out there who may still be in the suffering stage and, like me, do not want to take medication to cope. I will share a few things that did help me on this path of suffering. I first want to say; there is nothing wrong with anyone who decided to take medication to cope with his or her loss. As I stated previously, each person is different, and I strongly feel we all should do what's best for them and their health. I am sharing my experience and alternatives to medication. These alternatives do not solve things, but provide a way to prolong the decision to take medication if needed. I also will say talk to your doctor and follow his or her lead, as they would be the best person to understand your medical needs. The first thing I had to do was to truly mentally let go of my daughter. I had to release her from my fantasy world of believing she was not truly gone. I am still struggling with this step. As for other suggestions, taking walks in the park, the mall, any place that would allow me to clear my head, and yes, even walk and cry. Take a friend on these walks and talk about goals, dreams, or just girly stuff to take your mind off of your loss. Try changing your diet as well; eating right helps build energy, so when you walk, it will hopefully allow you to rest better at night. Also, find a therapist or a good friend who will allow you to vent when you need to and cry without judging or making you feel like you are insane. Another thing I did was get involved with organizations that I was able to meet people going through what I was going through. Talking to other women who understand your pain is so satisfying as well.

There is a time that the suffering will become numb to you and you are able to cope and deal with it better. Does it go away; in my opinion, no it never goes away. You learn to adjust and find room to carry the pain with you daily without feeling as if you are losing your mind. However, find the best way for you to cope and deal with the pain and, remember, our love ones have left this earth, but they are watching us, and it makes them sad to see us in pain and suffering. Therefore, do it for them if you can't find the strength to do it for yourself or your family. My daughter left a little girl behind, and my youngest son was terribly close to her as well. I wake up every day and put one foot in front of me and find ways to cope and means to have a more genuine smile because they need me to keep pushing and be there for them. When I see myself drifting into the depression hole, I mentally picture my son's face, and my granddaughter's face, and I keep pushing. I straddle the fence of depression daily, and one good thing I am aware of is that it's a daily fight I have that I will not allow it to take control over me. Once I finally reached this point of awareness, things became easier, and the suffering became less of a burden. Find your focus point, and you too can release some of the pain and stop suffering.

3 JOURNEY

Yes, the journey of grieving starts immediately; however, I never felt present with my journey until about a year or two. The first year, I felt like I was in a fog. I was present most of the time, but emotionally checked out about 99% of the time. The first 6 months after I took the medication prescribed to me (but not as prescribed – I would skip dosages because I really didn't want to take the medication). As I stated before, I went to see the doctor and I broke down crying. When she asked what the problem was, I managed to tell her I did not like the way the medicine made me feel and I wanted to stop taking it altogether. She had gone through something similar in her life, and she was all for me doing just that, and I was so relieved to finally have someone who understood. Therefore, since I made the decision not to take medications to help me process what I was fighting so hard not to process. I had to deal with all of the depression symptoms (too much sleep, not enough sleep, lack of appetite, weight gain, aggravation, frustration, anger, sadness, crying spells) all on my terms. This was definitely something difficult to tackle on my own, but I knew, in the long run, it would be a better decision for me and wanted to take each step slowly and deal with whatever came my way. Although I shared most of what I was going through with my husband and a select few friends or family, there were things I did not share and couldn't pull myself to share my thoughts at first out of embarrassment. I remember what a dear friend told me and I didn't understand until I had a moment of frustration and these words ran across my mind, "Your journey is your journey, and you will have to walk it alone 98% of the time, but just know you have people there willing to help when needed;" this statement became so powerful and meaningful after year one of dealing with the pain and hurt. No matter how frustrated I was at others for moving on with life like my daughter wasn't relevant anymore, or being upset at family and friends for not understanding when I wanted to not talk about my daughter, or being angry at the young lady who took her from me, the journey to healing is all about me. I finally realize this is a pain I will carry for the rest of my life and nothing no one could do or not do could change how I was feeling inside.

The first two years of my journey were a challenge. As I stated, I didn't want to take depression medication of any kind. As I went back to work and tried to become the person people were used to seeing, it was hard, but I managed to get through 45 minutes of crying to and from work daily and 8 hours a day in the office. The morning drive to work was always hard, but that was the time I would let out my tears before I had to bottle my feelings up to deal with my co-workers daily. Once I got through my day with the big smile everyone was expecting from me, I would get to my car and let out tears for 45 minutes on the way home to my family and not continue to let them know I was still struggling. I just didn't think anyone would understand how hard it was for me to move on. It was even harder watching everyone else go about life like nothing happened. I never missed a beat at work, and slowly, I started back being the OCD person at home. I cleaned, cooked, but still didn't have a desire to go out with friends or do much of anything. I still had my days that if I needed to do stuff, I could pull it together to go out and face the world. I dislike going to the grocery store because I was scared to bump into someone I knew and they would ask me that famous "How are you doing?" and I would lie and say oh I'm doing okay or I'm taking one day at a time. All while inside, I was kicking and screaming. I knew everyone meant well, but if I gave them the true answer "I am an emotional wreck inside, and I am not sure if I will ever be able to cope with the loss of my daughter," I would get the deer in the headlight stare because no one really wanted my true feelings. The questions asked were friendly, but wasn't meant to be truly open questions, it was one that people can say they ask me and it made them feel good during the meeting.

I started realizing, by myself, that this walk isn't fun, and I don't want to walk on this journey at all. I guess because 5 days a week I had to get up, get dressed, and go to work; I was forced to deal with life. It always seemed like I was standing still and everyone and everything was moving around me at warp speed and I couldn't catch up even if I tried. Therefore, I slept all weekend to avoid dealing with people. I would just come home from work on Friday and sleep all day and night, off and on until Monday morning. However, the one thing that would get me out of bed and moving was when we would get Chasity's daughter every other weekend. The weekends she was around gave me enough burst of energy that would give me the motivation I needed. She is so much like her mother; she would put a smile on my face. She brought joy to our home each time she walked through the door. I knew my life could not just stop because I had people who needed me to push through. Although I lost one child, I still had a 15-year-old at home to raise and who needed me as well. I also knew Chasity wanted me to be the loving person that she knew I was to her daughter. I only could be this person if I worked hard to find parts of that woman they looked up to and counted on. I was able to work through barriers and the obstacles, which lead me to the next part of the journey. As days went on, I became an insomniac during the week (I am still one now), and when my granddaughter wasn't at our home, I slept on the weekend. I would literally wake up on some days at 6:30 am and often would not go to bed until 4:00 or 5:00 am the next day and would still get up and go to work. I function like I had 8 hours of sleep. I continued this journey for a year or more. However, the more I threw myself into the Foundation business, the more I open myself up to doing more things.

The journey comes with a bigger price than anyone can ever imagine. Emotionally and mentally, it's a struggle to cope with the pain and still hold down a job, be a mother, wife, or friend to anyone. As I stated previously, I did not want to take any type of medications. However, as time went on and the lack of sleep I was getting, the different appetite ups and downs I was on, I started to contemplate taking medication several times. As the very doctor who agreed with my decision started seeing my body go through peaks and valleys and wanted me to take something after all. She was concerned that my hormones were malfunctioning because of what I was dealing with. However, based on her explanation of the medication, she couldn't tell me if I would ever get off the medication. I DID NOT want to take medication for the rest of my life to cover up what I was feeling. I politely declined again and continued on this journey without it and with determination and many prayers.

The journey for each of us could be a step-by-step, day by day, hour by hour, or even minute by minute. But it's each person's journey and walk to get through to the next stage of the grief. Each stage feels different and never one you would want to accept. I went from emotional to anger, to guilt, back to emotional and back to anger. I was angry with the young lady who took my daughter's life, to the friends who abandoned me while I was going through. However, that one friend's voice kept playing in my head, "I am here for you, but your journey is yours to take alone. I can't go with you on it, but I can be here to support you when you need me to do so." That, on many days, helped me push through. The days I didn't want to get out of bed to the days I refuse to talk about my daughter to anyone or look at pictures. I would smile and laugh one day, and within minutes, cry.

My journey wasn't easy to get to the point of acceptance. Acceptance was the place I didn't want to go to because I didn't want to accept that my daughter would never come back. I didn't want to live in the reality of her being gone. I knew I had to, but I fought it the entire way. I didn't want to be happy without her, I didn't want to take vacations without her, I didn't want to enjoy holidays without her, and I didn't want to live life without her. It wasn't fair, and I didn't want to accept it as being fair. But I knew that I had to do so because just as she counted on me in life, she counted on me in death to be the rock for her daughter as I was for her in her life.

It was a journey that humbled me when I didn't think I could be any humbler. It grew me to different spiritual level and place than I was before. I Thank GOD for the roller coaster ride I went on over the past 3 years. Although I begged to get off many days and each day is still a struggle, it was one that helped me grow as a woman and a mother. I have more emotions I will experience and days I will want to give in and think that self-medicating is the answer, but I will fight it and succeed.

I say this to anyone on the journey or anyone supporting a mother on the journey. Each person is different; listen to your body, talk to your doctors, and family members. But make the best decision for yourself that will make you feel as good as you can, but still allow you to walk your journey with pride.

4 NEW NORMAL

The new normal is all I heard the first year on repeat from everyone. I would think to myself, normal, my life would never be normal again. I got so tired of people making that statement some days I wanted to scream STOP; don't say that again to me. As the years past and after talking to different people I met through Mothers Against Drunk Driving ("MADD"), I began to understand what that statement meant to me. Remember, everyone's journey is different; therefore, everyone's new normal would be different. The journey never ends, just the process along the way changes and helps shape you into the place of your new normal.

Yes, I started the Foundation two months after my daughter's death, and I have been going strong since day one working. However, I didn't feel that was my new normal; I felt it was a way to keep her close to me and continue to grieve. As I stated previously, the grieving process was hard. I was working through the Foundation to stay busy and help me get out of bed, and during those nights, I was awake all night. I didn't know what to do with myself, and I felt like I was losing the battle of fighting against depression. I would go to networking functions for the Foundations and was unable to articulate the mission or even the backstory without breaking down crying in the middle of the conversation. I wanted the Foundation to succeed, and I desperately wanted to know my new normal that people kept telling me about. I started slowly, pushing myself more and more. I rehearsed a statement that I could say to people when they asked about the backstory of the Foundation, and soon, I was able to speak without crying. Things progressed in the networking field, and I started meeting several people who were inspired and wanted to help the cause. Although three years later, things are moving along and as each year passes, the events are becoming bigger and more noticeable in the community. I was still looking for my new normal.

One day recently (2017), as I was talking myself out of bed, I heard a voice say, "Mom, remember all the things we talked about doing, Let's do them." That day, I knew she was with me and understood what my next steps were to my new normal. I sat straight up in the bed and said Let's do them, baby girl. I felt for the first time a sense of all over the acceptance that my daughter was gone and nothing I did would ever bring her back in the physical form. She wanted me to live for her and carry her in my heart and my spirit. At that moment, I knew I was on my way to my new normal.

A new normal, to me, is the day you wake up and have an understanding of what direction your life will head in now that your child is no longer with you in the physical form. Remember, they will always be with us in spirit, but not the physical form. The thing I had to realize on my own was that my child is with me in spirit every day. No matter how crazy I may look to some, I can talk to her in my car, in my house, or write a simple letter in my journal. She will send me signs that she is still with me and give me hugs when the wind blows and give me a kiss when the sun shines on my face. I take this with stride, but I am still challenged with the acceptance and will continue making her proud through the Foundation.

I think when you are able to picture a life for yourself with the memories of your child, you can develop the new normal for yourself. I truly feel everyone's day will come, but at different times. Some discover their new normal within the first year, the second year, or the fifth year, but the ultimate goal is to find it for you. No one will understand your journey and what that new normal is for you, but you will know when you reach that point. Others will try to push you along faster than you want to go and you must push back and take your time. Yes, friends and family want to help, but they must understand that things will come for you in your time not their time. Don't stress yourself trying to meet the expectations of others, and if they are unable to accept you at the pace you are going, then remove them from your life. The pain of losing your child is one that only a mother or a mother who has experienced understands. However, surrounding yourself with friends and family, whether they have experience losing a child or not, but believe in you is a must. They will walk with you, listen to you, encourage you, support you, and be a shoulder to cry on when needed without ever questioning your process.

As I continued pushing forward with the Foundation we started as a means to help keep me busy from falling into a deep depression state, the Foundation has also become a motivation to share my story in hopes to continue to encourage myself and hopefully someone else. The fog I lived in for almost three years started to clear, and as the sun began to shine over me in my thoughts and dreams, it became clearer that my new normal should be moving forward.

Before my daughter passed, we discussed several trips we wanted to take and places we wanted to see; therefore, that morning, I heard her whisper in my ear, "Mom, remember all the things we talked about doing, Let's do them." I knew at that moment what I needed to do. As I prepare to send my youngest child off to college and I start to worry about me releasing him into this crazy world. I pray and ask that he is protected, and he stays focused on his goals. In the meantime, I started planning trips and made a promise to keep pushing for her because she is with me every day. I see the importance of me to once again stand strong not only for my family, but also for myself. I don't want to see her death be in vain. She didn't choose to leave this earth this early, and we didn't plan to bury her this early. However, we will work the mission of the Foundation to put smiles on under-served youth and their families in the community. I will do all of this in her name and honor because she would want to live on through the work and not through a negative memory of a night that stole her from us in the dark.

Therefore, when I'm down and feel like I can't put one foot in front of me, I will hear her voice in my ear, and it helps me push through. I realize my new normal does not mean I forget my pain, my journey, or my love for my daughter. It means I should continue to carry the pain and hurt with me daily as a reminder of her, what I've gone through, and push me to continue to overcome any obstacles in my way. As I am not an expert on depression, but I vowed in my prayer to my daughter I would not allow that to take me out or keep me from smiling, laughing, crying, or telling her story to anyone who would listen. I am ready to embrace my new normal and look forward to what my new future holds for me. I know no matter how I feel, my daughter is with me daily and she cheers me on and lets me know how proud she is about what I am doing to keep her memory alive for her daughter and love ones.

If I can leave one thing for the person who is reading this and not sure if they can go on without their loved one, YOU CAN!

Open Letters to my daughter:

(November 2014)

PLEASE, LORD, BRING MY BABY BACK HOME! I CAN'T ACCEPT THIS FOR HER!!!!!

(November 2014)

Dear Chasity,

Today, they tell me I have to say goodbye to you. I refuse to accept you're gone. Lord, please wake me up from this nightmare.

(December 2014)

Dear Chasity,

It has been a month since I received the news that you will not be coming home and I will never see your face again. I still do not want to accept that is my truth. Therefore, I sit every day not wanting to leave the house, praying that this is all a dream and you will walk through the door. I have so much anger and pain inside, and I do not know how to deal with it. I lost the only other connection to you, and that's your baby girl as well when she went to live with her dad. This is so hard for me, and I am not sure how I will ever accept you are gone. Your dad, Shamara, and Dre are heartbroken as well. But rather, some call it selfish or not, but I am so numb and fill with pain I can't be the strong one for anyone at this time. I pray every day that someone is able to step in to provide the shoulder for each of us to lean on because I cannot be that for anyone at this time. I don't know how to deal with my pain. PLEASE come home.   Love Mom

(January 2015)

Dear Chasity,

As I continue to sleep most of the days away, I heard God whisper in my ear to do something to keep your memory alive and to help me process the pain I feel. I had several people tell me I should start a Foundation in your name. I didn't think anything of it, but when I had that dream, I felt it was what you wanted as well. I followed God's lead and started The Chasity Taylor Foundation. Of course, we used your favorite color, purple, and Keaira got one of her friends to design a logo that is fitting for you. I hope this makes you proud. I was able to get Aunt Violet, Ashlea, Jarrod, and Ms. Myra on the board (I know you remember Ms. Myra lol). They are so happy to be a part that I think maybe it will be something good. I still miss you like crazy, and I still wait for the day you tell me it was not true, and you walk through the door.   Love Mom

(August 2015)

Dear Chasity,

We had our first event in honor of your memory and for the Foundation. I was so humble and overwhelmed with the number of families that came out; we were able to give away school backpacks and supplies, and it felt good. Your birthday is tomorrow, and although this day feels so good that we were able to bless the kids and put smiles on their faces, it hurts knowing you will not be here to celebrate your birthday. I am having a party for you, and I am going to try and be strong. I will try not to cry, but the pain is still as real as the day we found out you were never coming home.   I love and miss you like crazy.

Love Mom

(November 2015)

Dear Chasity,

I am still struggling with this and today makes it a year. I sit every night waiting for you to come through the door. I want to believe this is a terrible dream or a joke. You are not gone. The pain is just as real as the day I receive the news. This is still so hard. I love and miss you.

(November 2015)

Dear Chasity,

Today is Ari's 3rd Birthday, and she still asked where her mommy is. She doesn't understand, but we tell you are in heaven watching over her. It's so hard to see her come over and look around the house for you and still ask for you. We show her pictures and videos of you to her, and she just smiles and says, "That's my mommy." I wish you were here to see your baby girl grow up. She is just like you.

(December 2015)

Dear Chasity,

Another holiday without you, and I want to just sleep right through it, but I know no one will let me. I want to make all your favorites and pray you walk through the door calling my name like only you can. It just isn't the same without you. I'm praying to see Ari today and hope to see her smile will make today a little easier to deal with.

(January 2016)

Dear Chasity,

Everyone is making New Year resolutions, and I am still praying and hoping that I wake up from this nightmare and you are here with us. I love you and miss you!

(May 2016)

Dear Chasity,

As everyone prepares for Mother's day, I hate this day. I am sitting here wondering how do I celebrate being a Mother when I feel like I couldn't protect one of my children from harm. This is difficult; I just want to sleep today away as well.

(July 2016)

Dear Chasity,

It's a bittersweet day; today is Dre's birthday, and he will be the big 16. He is going to take his driver's license's test today. I wish you were here to share in the moment.

(August 2016)

Dear Chasity,

I know you have been watching over us, but today is the 2nd Annual Chasity Taylor weekend. I am getting ready to bless some youth with backpacks and school supplies to help them get ready for school. You loved school and did well, so this was the best way to keep your memory alive by helping others prepare to do well in school. I really miss you, and this pain still feels as real as day one.

(November 2016)

Dear Chasity,

Today marks the second year that you have been gone, and I cried like a big baby today. This doesn't seem to be getting better. The pain is so real, and I am not sure how people can move on with their life as if yours was taken too soon. I'm trying to overcome and accept things, but it's really hard.

JOURNAL

The best advice I ever received through my process of dealing with my lost was to write down my thoughts. In addition, write an open letter to my daughter. I am offering you the same advice and providing you a starting point. Write a letter to your son or daughter and release some of your feelings.

_____
_____
_____
_____
_____
_____
_____
_____
_____
_____
_____
_____
_____
_____
_____
_____
_____
_____
_____
_____
_____
_____
_____

A Mother's Love / A Mother's Pain

A Mother's Love / A Mother's Pain

A Mother's Love / A Mother's Pain

A Mother's Love / A Mother's Pain

ABOUT THE AUTHOR

Latricia N. Taylor was born and raised in Syracuse, NY. She graduated from Henninger Sr. High School in Syracuse, NY, obtained a Bachlor of Science in Paralegal Studies from Jones College in Jacksonville , FL. She went on to complete her Master's of Science in Administration of Justice and Security from the University of Phoenix. In addition, she completed all her coursework minus the dissertation in October 2014 in the doctoral degree program of Management in Organizational Leadership as well. Due to the death of her daughter, she was unable to complete the dissertation portion to complete the degree. She desires to finish what she started in honor of her daughter.

She has an intensive background in legal, business and as well as 20+ years' experience in health insurance. She is married and has three children (1 deceased), and three grandchildren. She is passionate about giving back to the community through he Foundation.

The Chasity Taylor Foundation, Inc.
P.O. Box 441104
Jacksonville, FL 32222
(904) 333-5076
chasitytaylorfoundation@yahoo.com
www.chasitytaylorfoundation.org
Facebook: The Chasity Taylor Foundation
Instagram: @chasitytaylorfoundation
Twitter: @CTFoundation823

A Mother's Love / A Mother's Pain

www.ingramcontent.com/pod-product-compliance
Lightning Source LLC
Chambersburg PA
CBHW061514040426

42450CB00008B/1607